WELCOME TO MOST LEGENDARY MATCHES

CH00482097

Lunar Press is a privately run publishing company which cares greatly about the accuracy of its content.

If you do notice any inaccuracies, or would like to discuss anything else about the book, then please email us at lunarpresspublishers@gmail.com.

Enjoy!

For my Grandad,

who taught me to love cricket.

Daniel

CONTENTS

INTRODUCTION

This book will take a look at 20 of the greatest international cricket matches that have ever been played. You will relive legendary recent matches such as England vs New Zealand in the 2019 World Cup final, as well as great games from the past such as the match between England and Australia in 1882, which caused The Ashes to come into existence.

This book is full of some of the greatest comebacks in history, as well as some of the most controversial moments, but before we get into that let's take a brief look at the history of cricket.

The origins of cricket are somewhat unknown, but are thought to date back as early as the 16th century. The name cricket stems from the Anglo-Saxon word 'cricc' which referred to a shepherd's staff. This is because shepherds were the first people believed to play cricket, and they used their 'criccs' as bats and the gates of cattle pens as the wickets!

The first English 'county teams' were formed in the second half of the 17th century, which gave rise to the games earliest 'professionals'. The first known women's game of cricket dates back to 1745 which was played in Surrey.

The first laws of the game were written in 1744, and later formalised by the Marylebone Cricket Club (MCC) in 1797. Cricket soon began to spread all across the world, with colonists introducing it to the West Indies and India, shortly followed by Australia in 1788, and then finally reaching New Zealand and South Africa in the early 19th century.

Fast forward to today and it is estimated that cricket is played by more than 30 million people, putting it at seventh in the world for most-played sport, and an astonishing second in the world for most-watched sport. Cricket quickly grew from a game played by shepherds in their fields with little to no rules, to being one of the most popular sports in the world!

Out of all the tens of thousands of cricket matches that have ever been played, these twenty stand out above the rest. Being called one of the GOATS (Greatest of all Time) is a very big claim to make, but these matches certainly live up to the label. There are shock upsets, crazy comebacks, and some of the best performances played on the big stages. These matches have all gone down in history, and will always be remembered as some of the greatest and most influential matches in the great sport of cricket.

THE GREATEST CHOKE

WORLD CUP SEMI-FINAL

AUSTRALIA
VS
SOUTH AFRICA
1999

PLAYED AT:
EDGBASTON, BIRMINGHAM,
ENGLAND

RUN UP TO THE GAME

Australia had only narrowly qualified for the semi-final stage of the World Cup after beating none other than South Africa in a crucial Super Six group match. Even this match had been a dramatic affair as South Africa's Herschelle Gibbs had dropped Australia's captain Steve Waugh when Australia were in trouble and in danger of being knocked out. Waugh went on to make 120 not out as his side won. His supposed response to Gibbs - "You've just dropped the World Cup" - went down in cricketing folklore due to its accuracy. Waugh later clarified that was not quite what he had said.

THE GAME

The semi-final, which followed the Super Six match just 4 days later, was even more dramatic. The match was close throughout as Australia were restricted to just 213 at a warm Edgbaston. Shaun Pollock returned the outstanding figures of 5-36 for South Africa as Australia One-Day International Great Michael Bevan top-scored with 65 and helped rescue his side from 68-4 with Waugh, who made 56.

South Africa progressed steadily in their run chase, but were left in a spot of bother after Jacques Kallis' departure to man of the match Shane Warne for 53. Pollock, who had been batting well, was yorked by a wonderful delivery from Damien Fleming for 20 soon after and it was again left to South Africa's powerful all-rounder Lance Klusener to get them across the line. Broad-shouldered, big-hitting, and sporting a chunky gold neckchain, Klusener was every inch the archetypal South African cricketer and had had a sublime tournament to date. He was to lose another of his partners in the penultimate over courtesy of a tight run out and then, dramatically, was almost out himself. Hitting another of his huge blows down to the long-on boundary, he was almost caught by Paul Reiffel. Reiffel misjudged the catch and ran in to take it only to parry the ball over the rope for six.

So far, so dramatic but the crowd hadn't seen anything like what was to come. It all came down to the last over with 9 runs needed to win for South Africa, Australia needing 1 wicket, and the swashbuckling Klusener on strike. What followed made cricketing history and resulted in the match being voted the best match of the 20th century by readers of CricInfo. The esteemed Wisden Cricketers' Almanack said "it must have been the best One-Day International of 1,483 so far played".

Klusener, on strike, scorched the first ball from Fleming through the covers for four. The second, from Fleming, he also scorched through the covers for four. Scores were level and it looked like being a relatively comfortable finish for the South Africans all things considered. However, due to Australia's marginally better record in the previous Super Six stage, a tie meant South Africa would lose so they still needed to score that precious extra run.

The third ball was mishit by Klusener and saw non-striker Allan Donald haring inadvisably up the pitch. There was never a run on. If Darren Lehmann hit the stumps from just a few feet away then South Africa would be out of the World Cup. He missed – about the easiest direct hit run-out chance you'll get in professional cricket but the pressure must have been intense. The fourth ball: Klusener again mishit, but this time he decided to run. Donald, perhaps mindful of his undue keenness the previous ball, didn't respond. Perhaps he didn't hear, perhaps he was too busy watching the ball. Either way, Klusener pretty much completed the run before Donald started his. Australia were quick to pounce and rolled the ball up to the wicket-keeper to take off the bails. Donald was nowhere near. He was out. Australia had won. South Africa had lost.

THE AFTERMATH

After the match, South Africa's coach resigned. He would later reveal that Donald was in tears after the result, along with many of his teammates. The match added further to the idea that South Africa crumbled, or "choked", under pressure in World Cups. They had lost crucial matches in 1992 and 1996 and would go on to make further blunders in 2003 and 2015. They have never won a World Cup. Australia went on to thrash Pakistan in the final and achieve a run of 34 World Cup matches without losing as they also won the 2003 and 2007 editions.

THE GREATEST TEST

THE ASHES 2005

AUSTRALIA
VS
ENGLAND
2ND TEST

PLAYED AT:
EDGBASTON, BIRMINGHAM, ENGLAND

RUN UP TO THE GAME

England had not won the Ashes since 1987 and Australia were still easily the number-one-ranked side in the world. However, England had enjoyed a stellar run of form in the lead-up, winning all 7 of their Test matches the previous summer and thrashing lowly Bangladesh immediately prior to the series. They had also thrashed Australia in the Twenty20 International at the start of the tour and run them close during the One-Day Internationals, including a tie in the tri-series final.

Therefore, hopes were high ahead of the first Test at Lord's. They were soon dashed. Aussie bowler Glenn McGrath had a stupendously good record at Lord's and added to it in taking 9 wickets in a comfortable win.

THE GAME

The match began in the worst possible way for Australia as they lost Lord's match-winner McGrath courtesy of a freak ankle injury.

Nonetheless, Australia still had momentum and a good replacement in Michael Kasprowicz. They also won the toss and put England into bat – a strategy in common with previously successful sides at this venue.

England, though, had other ideas and racked up for 407 at an impressively brisk rate, with Marcus Trescothick, Pietersen, and Andrew Flintoff each making fifties. Australia also scored at a fast rate and made 308 in their reply as opener Justin Langer top-scored with 82 and captain Ricky Ponting made 61.

This gave England a good-sized lead of 99 but they would need plenty more. Unfortunately for them, Shane Warne, who would go on to have one of the best series of his career, took 6 wickets for 46 runs and bowled unchanged from the seventh over from one end of the ground. Along the way, he bowled an outrageously good ball to Andrew Strauss that completely baffled the future England captain. As a result of Warne's brilliance, wickets fell regularly as one England batsman after another trudged back to the pavilion. Flintoff, though, would play a key role despite suffering from a shoulder injury that meant he was in obvious pain. He entered the fray at 72-5 with the lead only 171 following the departure of Pietersen but wickets continued to fall around him. He counter-attacked the best he could but the situation looked uncertain for the hosts as the penultimate wicket fell with the lead only 230.

Joined by Simon Jones, Flintoff stepped up a gear and took 33 runs off the 28 balls he faced from Australia's fastest bowler Brett Lee. Kasprowicz also bled runs and even Ponting setting 9 fielders on the boundary couldn't stop Flintoff hitting it over their heads for six. Eventually Warne came to Australia's rescue as Flintoff went for one big hit too many and was bowled. He and Jones had added a valuable 51 runs for the last wicket and set Australia 282 to win.

The fourth innings saw Flintoff again come to the fore. Australian openers Justin Langer and Matthew Hayden had progressed the score to 47 before Flintoff delivered what surely must rank as one of the best overs of all time. The second ball saw him deliver a leg-cutter that was too good for Langer and bowled him, bringing Australia's star batsman Ponting to the crease. Ponting was almost lbw first ball; almost caught at slip second ball; and almost lbw again third ball. With the crowd roaring, Ponting's fourth ball and the last in the over was easily left alone and passed harmlessly through to the wicket-keeper. Ponting would surely have breathed a sigh of relief but it was a no-ball. Flintoff had another go. This time he sent down another leg-cutter. It grazed the outside of Ponting's bat and Ponting was out for a duck.

England continued to take wickets and it began to look as though they might win easily as Australia found themselves 137-7 near the end of day 3. So close did they seem to be, in fact, that the extra half hour of play was allowed for them to try and finish off Australia that evening. Warne had other ideas and started counter-attacking alongside Australia's last recognised batsman Michael Clarke. The pair had advanced the score to 175 – little more than 100 away from victory – in what would turn out to be the last over of the day. England were beginning to get a bit frustrated by this point but there was more drama in store. Steve Harmison ran up to deliver the fourth ball of the 44th over and, in doing so, bowl what commentator Mark Nicholas would call "one of the great balls" as he completely outfoxed Clarke with a slower ball. Nicholas went on: "Given the moment, given the batsman and given the match, that is a staggering gamble that has paid off for Harmison. He bowled it perfectly."

England needed only 2 wickets for a series-levelling victory on the final day, while Australia still required 107 runs. The large numbers of spectators that came to the ground must have hoped that they would be present to celebrate an easy England win. They were nearly so so wrong.

Warne and Lee shaved 45 off the runs needed before Warne trod on his stumps and was out leaving 62 still needed with the last pair together. Ironically, McGrath's replacement Kasprowicz was actually a more accomplished batsman than the man he had replaced. He provided competent support to Lee and was dropped - a difficult chance to Simon Jones at third man - with 15 needed as an increasingly frantic England started to panic. Australia, mainly through Lee, edged closer and, for a second, as Lee smashed a cover drive with only four needed it looked like they might have won. A fielder was there and Australia could only get one run. Kasprowicz was on strike to Harmison with 3 runs required to the final ball of the 76th over. The delivery was short and reared unpleasantly at Kasprowicz. It hit his glove; hung in the air; and was snaffled by Geraint Jones. Umpire Billy Bowden raised his crooked finger. Kasprowicz was out. England had won by 2 runs. A disconsolate Lee dropped to his haunches and was quickly consoled by Flintoff in what was later widely regarded as one of the great acts of sportsmanship.

THE AFTERMATH

Ironically, had the match been played today it is likely Australia would have won. Kasprowicz should not have been given out by Bowden as the ball hit his glove when it was not in contact with the bat and had the decision been reviewed, as is possible now, it would have been overturned. There was no technology, however, to change the course of what would go on to become known as one of the greatest Test series of all time. The final 3 matches were all incredibly tense affairs as England eventually emerged as winners 2-1 to regain the Ashes after 16 years. They would lose them again about 18 months later by a margin of 5-0.

LARA'S AT HIS BEST

TEST MATCH 1999

AUSTRALIA
VS
WEST INDIES
3RD TEST

PLAYED AT:
KENSINGTON OVAL,
BRIDGETOWN,
BARBADOS

RUN UP TO THE GAME

The fortunes of the two sides differed markedly in the run-up to this series. Australia had beaten England again in an Ashes series, whereas West Indies had been whitewashed 5-0 in South Africa. West Indies skipper Brian Lara had led a player revolt over pay and conditions prior to that series and after leading his side to a humiliating loss in the first Test of this series – including them being bowled out for their lowest ever total of 51 – there were calls for his sacking as captain. He led a remarkable against-the-odds victory in the second Test, scoring 213 to level the series ahead of the third Test – one that was to be one of the greatest games of all time.

THE GAME

Australia started poorly after winning another coin toss, slipping to 36-3 courtesy of West Indies fast-bowling greats Curtly Ambrose and Courtney Walsh. However, captain Steve Waugh and future captain Ricky Ponting instigated a stunning fightback by hitting centuries to help Australia make an imposing 490.

West Indies then quickly slipped to 98-6 and the match looked to be over as a contest. Opener Sherwin Campbell and wicket-keeper Ridley Jacobs responded with a brilliant fightback and a stand of 153 for the seventh-wicket. Jacobs was finally out for 68, giving Ponting a rare Test wicket, while Campbell made 105 as West Indies were all out for 329.

This still put Australia in a very strong position with a lead of 161 and the heads of the West Indies bowlers could easily have dropped. Walsh, though, dismissed Matthew Elliott for his third duck of the series on the second ball and took 5-39 to help bowl Australia out for 146.

The West Indies target of 308 was still a stiff one for the fourth innings of a Test match against a very fine Australian bowling attack, that included 2 of the all-time greats in Glenn McGrath and Shane Warne. Openers Campbell and Adrian Griffith began well with a partnership of 72, but wickets tumbled thereafter and West Indies found themselves seemingly out of the game at 105-5.

It was again down to Lara, fresh off the back of his stupendous double-century in the previous match. He found good support from doughty left-hander Jimmy Adams and dominated a partnership of 133 that took West Indies to 70 runs away from victory. Australian heads were dropping, but McGrath bowled Adams for 38 and quickly dispensed with Jacobs and Nehemiah Perry to leave Australia just 2 wickets away and West Indies still 60 runs short.

Lara, by this point, had completed his century but was rapidly running out of partners. He found a useful ally in the form of Ambrose who doggedly occupied the crease as Lara scored runs at the other end against a tiring McGrath and the other increasingly exasperated Australian bowlers. More drama ensued as, with just 7 runs needed, Lara edged Jason Gillespie to Ian Healy behind the wicket. Healy dived to his left, in front of Warne at slip, to take the catch but failed to cling on. Everything seemed to be going West Indies' way. Had Australia just dropped the match?

Just 1 run later, however, Australia were back in the match as Gillespie finally ended Ambrose's stay at the crease at 39 balls. With 6 still needed, West Indies had the uninspiring figure of Walsh to rely on to face the rest of Gillespie's over. Walsh is one the greatest fast bowlers ever but one of the worst batsmen. The remainder of Gillespie's over included a no-ball and a wide to prolong the drama and add to Walsh's agony. The runs ticked down slowly until the scores were level and it was all over to Lara. Waugh brought the field up to make scoring the single as difficult as possible but Lara scorched one of his trademark drives through the covers and raised his arms aloft. West Indies had won by the merest of margins after one of the greatest Test match finishes of all time and had a 2-1 lead in the series ahead of the final Test. Lara finished on 153 not out.

THE AFTERMATH

West Indies would go on to lose the final Test at Antigua by 176 runs with yet another century from Lara, this one off only 82 balls, unable to prevent holders Australia from retaining the Frank Worrell Trophy as they have for an unbroken period stretching back to 1995.

BOTHAM'S ASHES

THE ASHES 1981

AUSTRALIA
VS
ENGLAND
3RD TEST

PLAYED AT:
HEADINGLEY, LEEDS, ENGLAND

RUN UP TO THE GAME

England and Australia were only mediocre Test sides in 1981 but that took nothing away from the magic of an Ashes series. England, in particular, had had a dismal run of form leading into this series under the captaincy of Ian Botham. Botham's 12-Test run as skipper would end without a win after defeat in the first Test of this series and a draw in the second, in which he made a pair of ducks. Mike Brearley, possibly England's best ever captain despite being a relatively poor Test batsman, was recalled ahead of the 3rd Test with England desperately in need of a win.

THE GAME

Brearley's tenure as captain looked like continuing where Botham's had left off as Australia dominated the first 3 days of the match. Australian opener John Dyson made a patient century to set up an imposing total on a difficult pitch. His 234-ball 102 laid the ground work for a score of 401-9 before Australian skipper Kim Hughes, who himself made 89, declared the innings closed. Botham, relieved of the captaincy, took 6-95 off almost 40 overs but the remainder of England's bowlers were uninspiring.

Australia's bowlers made much better use of the conditions and bowled England out for a paltry 174 despite Botham starring again, this time in making 50 off only 54 balls. Aussie seamers Dennis Lillee, Terry Alderman, and Geoff Lawson shared the 10 wickets to fall as England fell away badly from 78-3 at lunch to be all out by tea. Australia were then left frustrated by the poor light and the decision of the umpires to take the players off the field and could only take 1 England wicket after asking them to follow-on before the end of the day.

The fourth day dawned and it soon looked as though Australia would wrap the match up quickly. England collapsed to 135-7 – still 92 runs away from making Australia bat again – before one of the most remarkable turnarounds in cricket history began.

Botham was joined at the crease by Graham Dilley and was outscored by him for a time. Dilley drove powerfully over the fast outfield and collected boundaries as England reached tea on 176-7. Both men had played with great freedom and the many shots that went where they were intended were interspersed by plenty that didn't as they rode their luck. Dilley and Botham put on 117 in 80 minutes for the eighth-wicket before Dilley finally succumbed to Alderman for 56 off 75 balls.

Chris Old then joined Botham and watched him play a magnificent lofted drive for six that produced one of the greatest pieces of cricket commentary from Richie Benaud: "Don't bother looking for that, let alone chasing it. It's gone straight into the confectionary stall and out again." A little later, Botham smashed a cut shot for four to bring up his hundred in 157 minutes. Soon after, he lost Old for 29 and England's lead was still under 100.

The unlikely batting figure of Bob Willis then joined Botham. Botham sensibly took much of the strike and pressed England's lead up to 124 by the end of the fourth day.

England began day 5 still needing plenty more runs but didn't get many. Willis soon edged Alderman behind to end the innings at 356. Australia would need only 130 to win and it looked as if Botham's stupendous 149 not out might be in vain.

That was soon even more the case as Brearley's decision to open the bowling with Dilley and Botham in order to capitalise on any confidence they may have built up backfired. Australia progressed to 56 for the loss of only Graeme Wood as Dyson again took root. Willis, though, produced one of the great spells of fast bowling.

Cricket writer Christopher Martin-Jenkins wrote that Willis "bowled at fierce pace to a shorter length and a straighter line than in the first innings." By lunch Australia were 58-4 and then, soon, 75-8, but there was still more drama to come.

Lillee and Ray Bright took the score to 110 before Lillee became Willis' seventh victim when he was caught by Mike Gatting. Australia needed 20 to win and Alderman was soon edging a catch to slip. He was dropped and then dropped again 2 balls later. Surely England weren't going to throw it all away? No fear, Willis was here. He clean bowled Bright and England had won a match they never should have done by 18 runs.

THE AFTERMATH

England went on to win the series 3-1 and it would become known as Botham's Ashes as he was named man of the match in both the 4th and 5th Tests and also take 6-125 in the drawn 6th Test. The Headingley Test itself would be repeatedly replayed during rain breaks over the subsequent decades, particularly in the 1990s and 2000s when it looked as if England might never win another Ashes series. Australia would regain the Ashes in 1983 but then lose them again in 1985 and 1987 before winning 8 successive series.

SHRUBSOLE'S BEST

WORLD CUP FINAL

ENGLAND WOMEN VS INDIA WOMEN 2017

PLAYED AT:
LORD'S, LONDON, ENGLAND

RUN UP TO THE GAME

The 2017 World Cup had already been a big step forward for women's cricket before England and India had even bowled a ball at Lord's. The final at the Home of Cricket had sold out weeks previously and the TV audience was already up by 80% on the total 4 years earlier. This had all be underpinned by increased professionalism in the women's game with all of the players on all 8 of the competing teams now fully professional.

India had caused the first upset of the tournament by beating hosts England in the 1st round of fixtures. England, though, won their 6 remaining group games to top the table. They then won a nail-biting semi-final against South Africa with Anya Shrubsole hitting the winning runs with just 2 balls to spare.

India qualified as 3rd in the group to set up a semi-final against defending champions Australia. Harmanpreet Kaur was the undoubted star of that match with a wonderful knock of 171 off 115 balls and India won by 36 runs.

Ahead of the final, England were on the hunt for their 3rd World Cup triumph, while India had never lifted the trophy.

THE GAME

England's captain Heather Knight won the toss and elected to bat. Her openers Lauren Winfield and Tammy Beaumont laid a solid foundation despite the best efforts of Indian veteran Jhulan Goswami who sent down 5 overs at a cost of only 9 runs. Both departed in fairly quick succession and were soon followed by Knight to leave England on 63-3.

Sarah Taylor and Nat Sciver then came together and rebuilt the innings. The score had reached 133 without further loss when Goswami was reintroduced to the attack by her skipper Mithali Raj. Goswami had Taylor caught for 45 and Sciver sent packing for 51 either side of dismissing Fran Wilson for a golden duck. Her second spell had yielded 3-14 to give her match figures of 3-23 and reduce England to 168-6.

With Goswami finished, England's all-rounders set about adding as many runs as they could in the final overs. Katherine Brunt and Jenny Gunn put on 32 before Brunt was run-out for 34 off 42 balls. Gunn and Laura Marsh then added another 32 to take their side to 228-7 off 50 overs.

The total was probably below-par but runs on the board in the final are always worth more; or so goes the old adage.

India lost opener Smriti Mandhana in Shrubsole's first over for a duck but soon began to put together a partnership. The score had reached 43 when Raj was run-out, but Punam Raut and Kaur, fresh off her semi-final exploits, set about breaking the back of the total. They had added 95 and got the runs required down to 91 off 100 balls when Kaur was caught for 51.

A belligerent Veda Krishnamurthy then entered the fray and started to try to up the scoring rate. England had bowled tightly and kept themselves in the match but Krishnamurthy and Raut took India closer to their first title. Raut was finally dispatched for 86 off 115 balls by Shrubsole to give England an opening. India needed only 38 runs from 43 balls at this point with plenty of wickets in hand.

Shrubsole, though, seized her moment. The over after Alex Hartley had bowled the surprisingly promoted Sushma Verma second ball, she got the key wicket of Krishnamurthy for 35 and then clean-bowled Goswami for a duck. India were now 201-7.

Shikha Pandey and Deepti Sharma inched their side a little closer and had India needing only 11 off 16 balls when Pandey set off for a suicidal single and was run-out. India's quest for 11 off the final the 2 overs got off to a terrible start when Sharma was caught off Shrubsole. Three balls later, Rajeshwari Gayakwad was bowled by woman of the match Shrubsole and India were all all out 10 runs short of their target.

THE AFTERMATH

Shrubsole's figures of 6-46 were the best in a World Cup final. Her captain told the BBC: "Anya Shrubsole, to win us a game, under huge pressure - it's amazing. India batted brilliantly, they made it really hard for us. We knew if we took it deep, we had the bowling, and if we could hold our nerves. I thought about taking Anya off and I'm really glad I kept her on!"

Shrubsole announced her retirement from international cricket in 2022, shortly after England had failed to defend their title with a 71-run loss to Australia in the final of the 2022 World Cup.

India failed to make the semi-finals of the 2022 edition but women's cricket in the country continues to grow and a women's edition of the multi-billion dollar Indian Premier League is set to debut in 2023.

THE TIED TEST

TEST MATCH 1960

AUSTRALIA
VS
WEST INDIES
1ST TEST

PLAYED AT:
THE GABBA, BRISBANE, AUSTRALIA

RUN UP TO THE GAME

The 1950s had seen some fairly turgid games of cricket. Cricket writer Rob Steen later wrote that of the "11 dullest Tests in history, 10 took place between 29th January 1954 and 5th December 1958." There had also been issues with chucking from bowlers and riots by crowds. Perhaps West Indies' first full-time black captain Frank Worrell and Australia's Richie Benaud were aware of all this as they embarked on one of the most enthralling series of all time – one that began with one of the most thrilling matches of all time.

THE GAME

Interestingly the scoring rate for the series was actually slightly lower than the average for the time but this was more than made up for by the closeness of the matches. The first Test at The Gabba did see West Indies begin in relatively brisk fashion. They closed day one on 359-7 thanks to Garry Sobers, who made 132 in 174 minutes. Worrell and Joe Solomon each made 65 and Wes Hall then added 50 from number 10 – one of only two times in his career that he would reach the milestone – as the tourists were all out for 453 on the second day.

By stumps on the second day Australia had replied strongly with 196-3 courtesy of 92 from Bob Simpson and 57 from Colin McDonald. Day three saw Australia march into a commanding position thanks to Norm O'Neill. He saw them to 469-5 at one point before Hall entered the fray and triggered a collapse of 5-36 on his way to figures of 4-140. O'Neill was last man out with the score on 505. His score of 181 would remain the highest of his 42-Test career.

Australia, therefore, had a lead of 52 heading into the penultimate day. West Indies batted for all of day 4 and were all out for 284 early on the final day after falling away badly from a position of 210-4. Worrell top-scored for them with 65, while Alan Davidson added to the 5-135 he had taken in their first innings with 6-87.

Australia would need 233 to win in the fourth innings in what would turn out to be 69 8-ball overs. They looked to be out of it after lunch as Hall took 4 wickets to help reduce them to 92-6. However, Benaud and the excellent Davidson combined to take the score to 226 without further loss of a wicket. Their partnership of 134 was a record for Australia in Tests against the West Indies. Davidson, meanwhile, became the first man ever to record a match aggregate of 10 wickets and 100 runs in a Test.

The run rate was always a lingering concern for Australia and with just 7 needed the drama began in earnest. Maybe it was excellent fielding or maybe it was increasing desperation on the part of the Australians but 3 batsmen would be run out over the next few balls. There would also be a dropped catch and a missed run-out. Australia should never have been in trouble with so few runs required but Davidson's run out courtesy of a sharp piece of fielding from Solomon left Australia with 6 to get from the final 8 balls and upped the panic.

The first ball of the final over was a leg-bye, while the second saw the set batsman Benaud caught behind, off Hall, to end his innings at 52. The next ball was played back to the bowler by new man Ian Meckiff, while the fourth almost saw another run out as Meckiff and Wally Grout scrambled through for a bye to the wicket-keeper. Grout was dropped off the fifth ball by bowler Hall as a result of a mix-up with fielder Rohan Kanhai but managed another run to leave just 3 runs needed.

Ball six was struck to leg by Meckiff and was heading towards the boundary. Conrad Hunte picked up the ball but the batsmen were on their way back for the winning third run. Would they make it? The throw from Hunte was a good one and Grout was run out by a foot to leave the scores level with 2 balls left and 1 wicket remaining.

Number 11 Lindsay Kline hit the ball towards Solomon at square-leg and non-striker Meckiff set off for the winning run. For the second time in just a few minutes Solomon threw down the wicket and Meckiff was out.

The scores were level and Australia had no wickets left — the first time such a situation had ever happened in the 498 matches played over 84 years up until this point.

THE AFTERMATH

There has only been one other tied Test match to date — in 1986 — despite there now having been well over 2000 Test matches played.

As for the series itself, it was be an excellent one as mentioned. The fourth Test was a draw, with the home side 9 wickets down, while the fifth and deciding match was narrowly won by Australia to see them take the series 2-1.

West Indies were exceedingly popular tourists and were paraded through Melbourne in an open-top car where they were cheered by large crowds prior to their departure. Writer Jack Fingleton would later write a book on the series centred on the first Test aptly called The Greatest Test of All.

THE START OF A REMARKABLE JOURNEY

WORLD CRICKET LEAGUE LEAGUE DIVISION 5

JERSEY VS AFGHANISTAN 2008

PLAYED AT:

GRAINVILLE, ST SAVIOUR, JERSEY

RUN UP TO THE GAME

Cricket only really began to be played by an Afghanistan national team in the 1990s and, even then, due to war it was played by refugees in neighbouring Pakistan as the sport was banned by the ruling Taliban until 2000. The ICC only accepted the Afghanistan Cricket Federation as a member in 2001. It was from this backdrop of war that Afghanistan looked to win their first ever global tournament when they rolled up in the cricketing backwater of Jersey for Division 5 of the World Cricket League.

Afghanistan had been made to sweat on a place in the semi-finals after losing to Singapore but squeezed through on net run rate. They then beat Nepal and secured promotion to Division 4. This set up a final against hosts Jersey.

THE GAME

The match was an extremely low-scoring affair. Jersey won the toss and elected to bat and made a slow start. The score had reached 13 before Hasti Gul struck in consecutive overs. More wickets left Jersey on 25-4 before a slight fightback from Steve Carlyon and Jonny Gough took the score to 67 without further loss.

Tearaway quick Hamid Hassan then set about demolishing the rest of the batting line-up. He had Carlyon caught for 17 – the fact it had taken 84 balls demonstrated the excellence of the Afghan bowling and presumably the tricky nature of the pitch – and then Gough bowled for 23. Jersey were soon all out for a paltry 80 as Hassan ended with 4-27 and Gul 3-17.

The run chase then should have been an easy one for the Afghans. It was to be anything but. Former English county player Ryan Driver was to be their chief tormentor. He took 4 wickets as Afghanistan found themselves 42-7. Another wicket fell with the score on 62 when future Afghan skipper Asghar Stanikzai was lbw to Matt Hague for a painstaking 10 off 65 balls. Jersey were now arguably favourites as Afghanistan needed a further 19 with only their bowlers left to bat.

Bowling star Hasti Gul, however, found reliable support from Dawlat Ahmadzai and the pair moved the score towards their target. There was a moment of comedy when the score reached 80 as Gul's teammates charged onto the field to celebrate a win before realising the scores were only level. They would have to wait a further 4 balls before finally celebrating victory. Gul ended on 29 not out having hit the only 2 sixes of the match and 2 of his sides 4 fours.

THE AFTERMATH

What came next for Afghanistan would make this match more notable than it had been at the time. They would win both Division 4 and Division 3 of the World Cricket League to earn a place in the World Cup Qualifier. They didn't quite qualify, finishing 5th, but did secure One-Day International status and later qualified for the 2015 edition. They did qualify for the 2010 edition of the World T20 and also won the inaugural edition of the four-day Intercontinental Cup in 2010.

Afghanistan became a top-flight team for real when they made their Test debut in 2018. In the space of a decade they had gone from competing against the likes of Japan, Botswana, and the Bahamas in the World Cricket League to competing in a Test match against India. There have been a few bumps as the Taliban have taken over the country once again putting the prospect of playing a home Test on hold and further harming the prospect of a women's team playing regular cricket.

Jersey have also progressed, although not nearly as far, and have made it to the last 3 qualifying events for the T20 World Cup without coming close to qualifying for the main event.

INDIA BEAT THE UNBEATABLE

TEST MATCH 2001

AUSTRALIA
VS
INDIA
2ND TEST

PLAYED AT:
EDEN GARDENS, CALCUTTA,
INDIA

RUN UP TO THE GAME

Australia were on a world-record winning streak of 16 Test wins following an easy win in the first Test of the series in Mumbai. They were well on the way to becoming one of the greatest Test sides of all time and wanted to win for the first time in India since 1969 to conquer what is often seen as the final frontier for a great Test side.

India were already without leading spinner Anil Kumble due to a shoulder injury and went into the Calcutta Test further weakened by the absence of leading pace bowler Javagal Srinath after he picked up a finger injury in the Mumbai defeat. Their ever-opinionated former captain Bishan Bedi was lamenting the decline of Indian cricket and they were frantically scrabbling around trying to find a replacement spinner for Kumble.

THE GAME

Australia began the match where they had left off in Mumbai, easily dominating the first 2 sessions to reach tea at 193-1. Harbhajan Singh — who had struggled so much of late with accusations of chucking and disciplinary issues that he had been tempted to move to the US to become a truck driver — was failing in his mission to be a suitable replacement for Kumble despite captain Sourav Ganguly's insistence that he be selected for this series. That, though, would quickly change. Harbhajan had Matthew Hayden caught in the first over after tea and, a little later, took the first ever hat-trick by an Indian in Test matches. He dismissed Australian greats Ricky Ponting, Adam Gilchrist, and Shane Warne in successive deliveries as the visitors reached stumps at 291-8.

India were back in the match but Australia dominated day 2 and they soon looked to be out of it again. Steve Waugh made 110 as Australia recovered to make an imposing 445. India began steadily but lost 7 wickets in the final session to close on 128-8. They were soon all out for 171 despite VVS Laxman making 59 and Australia appeared to be on the way to extending their winning streak to 17 as they asked India to follow-on.

What followed next was remarkable: only 2 teams in the 100-year-plus history of Test cricket had ever won after being asked to follow-on. India began solidly, but at 115-3 with the dismissal of star batsman Sachin Tendulkar for only 10, they were still well behind. Ganguly and Laxman added 117 to take the score to 232 before the former fell 2 short of a determined half-century. Laxman reached his century before the end of the day as India closed on 254-4.

India began day 4 still 20 runs behind Australia, but the 14th March 2001 was to be a historic day in their Test history and even more so in the careers of VVS Laxman and Rahul Dravid. Amazingly, the pair batted all day without getting out and took the score to 589-4 at stumps – a lead of 315 runs. Early the next day both were out and received standing ovations from the huge Eden Gardens crowd. Laxman had made 281 – the highest Test score by an Indian and had hit 44 boundaries. Dravid was out for 180, having hit 20 boundaries. The pair had put on 376 runs – the highest fifth-wicket stand in India's Test history and their second highest for any wicket. India finally declared at 657-7 to leave Australia needing 384 to win in 75 overs to extend their winning streak. More realistically, they needed to bat out two and a half sessions for the draw.

They began well and the game looked to be heading for a draw at 166-3 with only 30 overs left to survive for Australia. However, Harbhajan again entered the fray. He had Steve Waugh and Ricky Ponting dismissed in the same over. In the next, Gilchrist became the first Australian to be dismissed for a king pair in Test cricket when Tendulkar, a somewhat infrequent bowler, had him lbw. Tendulkar also had Hayden leg before for 67 and Warne leg before for 0 to make it 174-8. Australia's ninth-wicket pair of Jason Gillespie and Michael Kasprowicz hung around for a while before Harbhajan dispatched the former for 6 off 38 balls. Glenn McGrath then surprised many by proving adept at batting for several overs. He and Kasprowicz took Australia to within 7 overs of a draw. Harbhajan finally ended McGrath's resistance at 12 as Australia were all out for 212. Harbhajan ended with incredible match figures of 13-196. He still lost out on the man of the match award to Laxman's 281.

THE AFTERMATH

India went on to win the third Test to take the series 2-1. Harbhajan took 15 wickets and was named man of the match and man of the series with 32 wickets across the 3 Tests. Incredibly, none of his teammates had managed more than 3 wickets in the series. The series kick-started Harbhajan's Test career and he would go on to become one of India's greatest ever bowlers.

Australia were still a great side. They won the following ODI series against India, would have another 16-game winning streak in Tests a few years later, and finally achieved success in a Test series in India less than 4 years later in 2004.

ENGLAND FINALLY WIN. JUST.

WORLD CUP FINAL

**ENGLAND
VS
NEW ZEALAND**

2019

PLAYED AT:
LORD'S, LONDON,
ENGLAND

RUN UP TO THE GAME

Neither New Zealand nor England had ever won the World Cup. The former had suffered defeat at the hands of hosts Australia last time out, while England had lost finals in 1979, 1987, and 1992. Last time they had hosted the World Cup, in 1999, they had suffered the ignominy of being knocked out before the official World Cup song had even been released for sale.

This time around, England were one of the favourites under their Irish-born captain Eoin Morgan, while New Zealand were also one of the top 50-over sides. Both sides suffered defeats during the lengthy group stage. England beat New Zealand to clinch their spot in the last four, while New Zealand only crept in ahead of Pakistan on the penultimate day of the group stage. Both teams won their respective semi-finals, with New Zealand again having the harder time, against India during a rain-affected match at Old Trafford.

THE GAME

Finals don't always produce close games, but this one was very much the exception as it proved virtually impossible to separate the two sides. It was also a fairly low-scoring affair as nerves, perhaps, overcame both sides' natural attacking instincts.

New Zealand won the toss, chose to bat, and struggled to a total of 241-8. Henry Nicholls hit a somewhat laboured but important 55 off 77 balls from the top of the order, while Tom Latham hit 47 off 56 balls. England's bowling was economical and effective, with Liam Plunkett and Chris Woakes ending with 3 wickets apiece.

England were favourites at the halfway stage but the old adage of scoreboard pressure in a final bore true. They were reduced to 86-4 in the 24th over, but battled back courtesy of a century stand between star all-rounder Ben Stokes and Jos Buttler. Buttler, though, was out with the score on 196 for 59 to leave Stokes and the bowlers to get 46 off the last 5 overs – a stiff ask.

Stokes handled the situation well, not asking too much of the other batsmen, and got the situation down to 15 off the final over. New Zealand were probably favourites at this stage – even more so after Trent Boult prevented Stokes from scoring off the first 2 balls. Finally, Stokes got the ball away, smoking a six and then benefitting from fortune, overthrows, and controversy to get another six runs and put England firmly back in charge and leave them needing 3 to win off the final 2 deliveries.

The penultimate ball yielded a run-out and 1 run as Stokes desperately tried to keep himself on strike for the final ball but ended up running out Adil Rashid in the process. The last ball, with 2 needed, was almost a carbon copy as Mark Wood was run out haring back for the winning second. He was out and the match was a tie. For the first time, there would be a super over to decide the winner of a World Cup.

There was more drama to follow. England made 15 from their over – as we have seen, a challenging score. New Zealand started wonderfully, benefitting from a wide and a six from Jimmy Neesham to require just 7 from 4 balls. There were 4 runs off the next 2 balls and 1 run from the fifth to again leave 2 to win off the final ball.

1 run would be no good for New Zealand as England had hit more boundaries during their innings and that would be good enough for them to win if the super over was also tied. You can probably guess what happened. Batsman Martin Guptill hit the ball out to deep mid-wicket, set off for 2 and was run out coming back for the second. England had won a spectacular final, after both the main match and the super over had been tied, on number of boundaries hit.

THE AFTERMATH

There was criticism from some quarters of using boundary count to decide the match as fewest wickets lost had historically been used to decide a lot of tied one-day games. In any event, the International Cricket Council decided that, in future, teams would play as many super overs as possible until a winner emerged.

Of more relevance was the decision of umpire Kumar Dharmasena to award England 6 runs instead of 5 in the final over when the throw from Martin Guptill hit Stokes' bat and rebounded for 4. As Stokes and his partner had not crossed for the second run when Guptill threw the ball they should not have been credited with it.

New Zealand accepted their defeat with remarkably few complaints given the circumstances. England were welcomed to the Prime Minister's residence in Downing Street and congratulated by the Queen. Several players, including man of the match Stokes, were honoured in the New Year's Honours List.

The match was shown on free-to-air TV, unusual for a cricket match in England, and was viewed by 8.3 million people, making it one of the most watched broadcasts of the year and making the games' administrators usual insistence on sticking matches on pay TV channel Sky Sports seem even more ridiculous than usual.

"ONE OF THE GREATEST GAMES IN TEST HISTORY"

THE ASHES 2022

ENGLAND WOMEN VS AUSTRALIA WOMEN ONLY TEST

PLAYED AT:
MANUKA OVAL, CANBERRA, AUSTRALIA

RUN UP TO THE GAME

The Women's Ashes is played in a slightly different way to the men's. For the 2021-22 Ashes in Australia, the women played 3 Twenty20 games, one Test, and 3 One-Day Internationals, with 2 points available for a win in each of the one-day games and 4 points available for a win in the Test match (2 points for a draw).

The 3 Twenty20 games had been badly impacted by rain, with Australia winning the 1st easily but the next 2 being rained off. The points tally stood at 4-2 to Australia heading into the Test match. A draw would mean England would probably have to win all 3 games in the ODI series if they were to regain the Ashes from Australia for the 1st time since 2015.

THE GAME

England's captain Heather Knight won the toss and chose to ask the opposition to bat 1st on the pitch in Australia's capital. The early rewards were the wickets of Australian wicket-keeper Alyssa Healy for a duck and Beth Mooney for just 3. A partnership of 169 for the 4th wicket between Rachael Haynes and Aussie skipper Meg Lanning then put the home side in charge. Both fell just short of centuries, but fifties from Tahlia McGrath and

Ashleigh Gardner allowed Australia to declare on 337-9. Katherine Brunt was England's standout bowler with 5-60.

England's innings was dominated by their captain. Knight, perhaps disappointed with the result of her decision at the toss, made an unbeaten 168, one of the greatest innings in women's Test history, from number 3 in her side's total of 297. The next best score was 34 from tail-ender Sophie Ecclestone as Ellyse Perry led the way for Australia's bowlers with 3-57.

Australia then began their 2nd innings with a lead of 40 runs and again lost 2 early wickets. This time it was Mooney who led the recovery alongside Perry; the pair taking the score past 100. Again, useful contributions from McGrath and Gardner advanced the score further. Australia had reached 216-7 in the afternoon session when Australian captain Lanning decided to take the aggressive decision to declare. Remember, a draw would have put Australia in a very strong position ahead of the ODI series, but Lanning wanted to win the Ashes here and now and was probably aware that England would have to score the highest ever total in the 4th innings of a Test match if they were to win.

England began positively and were clearly going for the win. Openers Lauren Winfield-Hill and Tammy Beaumont added 52 in 14 overs to get things going and there was a more-than-useful 48 off 54 balls from

Knight. Nat Sciver and Sophia Dunkley were batting well during their 4th wicket partnership and had the equation down to 45 off 10 overs. England were strong favourites at this stage and Lanning must have been beginning to question her decision.

Dunkley had needed the decision review system to save her from a 1st ball duck but looked well in the mood to capitalise on the reprieve, hitting boundaries with abandon. A couple of tight overs resulted in the dismissal of Sciver for 58 off 62 balls. This would be the first of 3 crucial wickets for Annabel Sutherland that brought Australia back into the contest. Dunkley was also dispatched by Alana King for 45 off 32 balls and England were soon left needing 13 off 15 balls with 3 wickets in hand.

They were still favourites but more tension was in store. Anya Shrubsole was run-out, while King looked to have Charlie Dean caught next ball, only for the umpire to request the assistance of the TV umpire to check for a no-ball. Agonising seconds followed before Dean was adjudged out and England suddenly had only 1 wicket left and still needed 13 to win. The last-wicket pair of Ecclestone and Kate Cross elected to go for the draw and this was achieved. England ended on 244-9, both sides surely experiencing a mixture of relief and disappointment.

THE AFTERMATH

Lanning admitted that she felt "like we might have got away with one a little bit." Sciver said she felt "more sad than happy" following the result. The Test was widely hailed as one of the greatest of all time, with former Australian player Holly Ferling writing on Twitter that: "We have witnessed one of the greatest games in Test history."

Australia had the last laugh as they won all of the 3 ODIs that followed to retain the Ashes by the seemingly comfortable margin of 12 points to 4.

BIRTH OF AN ICON

TOUR OF ENGLAND

ENGLAND VS AUSTRALIA 1882

PLAYED AT:
THE OVAL, LONDON, ENGLAND

RUN UP TO THE GAME

The Australian and English sides regularly toured each other, playing a series of first-class games against a variety of teams before Test matches were even a thing. For example, on this 1882 tour, Wisden records several matches played by the Australians against county teams, as well as games against the likes of Gentlemen of England, Orleans Club, and Scotland. According to Steven Lynch, the Australians played an astonishing 33 first-class games, and 5 others, on their 1882 tour, losing only 4. Fred Spofforth took an incredible 157 wickets, while captain Billy Murdoch topped the run charts with 1582 runs.

Wisden also notes that, prior to the match at The Oval, the English side was far better on paper than their Australian counterparts according to the averages from the 1882 season to date. In other words: England were strong favourites.

THE GAME

Indeed, that soon looked very much the case as Australia were bowled out for just 63 in 80 4-ball overs after winning the toss and electing to bat. Only 3 batsmen reached double figures, all of them taking their time, and

Jack Blackham top-scoring with 17. Opener Alec Bannerman almost joined them but "was splendidly caught by [WG] Grace at point, left hand, low down, having been in an hour and 5 minutes for 9 runs." Dick Barlow took 5-19, while Ted Peate returned 4-31.

The legendary Doctor WG Grace, a true icon of the Victorian age with his long beard and astonishing cricketing feats, then walked out to open but could manage only 4 before departing to Fred "The Demon Bowler" Spofforth. Spofforth is another that has gone down in cricketing history as a legendary figure of the game and is credited as having been able to bowl with incredible accuracy, stamina, and skill. He took 7-46 as England were bowled out for 101 with George Ulyett top-scoring with 26.

England, then, had a lead of 38 on first innings. Opener Hugh Massie led the way in knocking these off quickly. Wisden records that "30 went up after about 28 minutes' play, two bowling changes having been tried... It was not until the score reached 66 that loud applause greeted the dismissal of the great hitter, bowled leg stump [for 55] by [Allan] Steel." The remainder of the Australians' innings followed a similar pattern to those in the match thus far. Murdoch's 29 was the next best score as the "Colonists" were all out for 122, Peate again taking 4 wickets.

There was a moment of controversy that may have served to spur the Australians on in their bowling effort later. Sammy Jones was run out by Grace when he meandered out of his ground after assuming the ball was dead after completing a run. Wisden reports: "Several of the team spoke angrily of Grace's action, but the compiler was informed that after the excitement had cooled down a prominent member of [the] Australian eleven admitted that he should have done the same thing had he been in Grace's place."

The match looked lost for Australia following their collapse but Spofforth was not deterred and is reported to have said to his teammates: "Boys, this thing can be done." He took 2 wickets in as many deliveries with the score on 15, but England's Grace and Ulyett took the score past 50 without further loss and they looked well on their way to reaching their paltry target of 85. Ulyett, though, was dismissed for 11 courtesy of a "very fine catch at the wicket" with Grace soon following him back to make it 53-4.

England were becalmed as 12 successive maiden overs were bowled and the tension mounted. Runs, and wickets, continued to trickle in, the latter mainly due to Spofforth, and both teams edged closer to their respective targets. Spofforth got his seventh wicket when he dismissed Bunny Lucas for 5 to make it 75-8 with England still needing 10 runs. The tension was incredible but Harry Boyle picked up the last 2 wickets for the addition of only 2 more runs. Australia had won by 7 runs. Spofforth ended with match figures of 14-90, which would easily end up as his best figures from his 18 Test matches.

THE AFTERMATH

The game's legacy is even more important than the game itself was. It gave birth to the Ashes, cricket's — perhaps sport's — greatest contest. Mock obituaries appeared in both Cricket: A Weekly Record of The Game and The Sporting Times. The latter included the famous phrasing:

"In Affectionate Remembrance
of
ENGLISH CRICKET,
which died at the Oval
on
29 August 1882,
Deeply lamented by a large circle of sorrowing friends and acquaintances

----

R.I.P.

N.B. — The body will be cremated and the ashes taken to Australia."

England's captain Ivo Bligh picked up on the concept of regaining "those ashes" ahead of their next tour to Australia and is said to have been presented with a small red urn containing the ashes of a burnt bail to bring back with him following his side's 2-1 win. The small red urn now resides in the museum at Lord's.

"The Ashes" would eventually become the name for the Test series between England and Australia which is now played twice every 4 years for that little red (now very fragile) urn.

THE FIRST WORLD CUP

WORLD CUP FINAL

WEST INDIES VS AUSTRALIA 1975

PLAYED AT:
LORD'S, LONDON,
ENGLAND

RUN UP TO THE GAME

The limited-overs game was still in its infancy as 8 teams converged on England in 1975 for the inaugural World Cup (the completely separate women's event had been held in 1973, so technically this was the second). The matches were all 60 overs per side, were all played in whites using a red ball, and there was not a floodlight in sight.

England and the West Indies were the top two sides in the rankings heading into the event. The former won all 3 of their group games easily but lost a very low-scoring contest against Australia in the semi-final. The West Indies had scraped past Pakistan in one of their group games to set up a semi-final against New Zealand which they won comfortably. They had beaten Australia in their group game so were firm favourites heading into the final at the Home of Cricket in front of a sell-out crowd.

THE GAME

Australia invited the West Indies to have first use of the Lord's track and soon had them in a spot of bother at 50-3, with Roy Fredericks standing on his wicket as he hit Dennis Lillee for 6. Clive Lloyd and Rohan Kanhai then came together to put the West Indies in a strong position. Lloyd made the most of being dropped on 26 to make an 82-ball century and dominate a stand of 149. Kanhai fell from 55 shortly after Lloyd's departure for 102 but Keith Boyce hit 34 and Bernard Julien 26 not out to leave the West Indies with a strong total of 291-8 off their 60 overs. Gary Gilmour followed up his match-winning 6-14 in the semi-final with 5-48.

Australia began their run chase steadily and reached 80-1. Viv Richards then struck with 3 run outs, each removing a set batsman and each benefitting from hesitant running on the part of the Australians. He had Alan Turner out for 40, Greg Chappell cut short on 15, and captain Ian Chappell sent packing for 60. The latter was a particularly important blow as it left Australia needing a further 130 runs from about 21 overs without their captain. They edged closer but lost wickets att crucial moments as the required run rate increased. When Lillee joined Jeff Thomson at the wicket as the last pair of batsmen and with 59 runs still needed off only 7 overs the game looked lost.

Amazingly, the two, not overly renowned for their batting, kept the game alive. With 3 overs to go the crowd streamed onto the pitch thinking the game was over when Lillee hit a no-ball from Vanburn Holder into Fredericks' hands at extra cover. They had failed to hear the umpire's call and thought Lillee was out. Fredericks attempted a run out but missed and the ball went into the crowd. Once the crowd had been dispersed the umpires deemed that Australia could have scored 2 runs – soon revised up to 3 after a protest from Thomson. It made little difference. Thomson soon became the 5th batsmen in the innings to be run out by a calm-headed Deryck Murray and the West Indies were winners of the match by 17 runs and the first winners of the World Cup. The match had provided thrilling entertainment for a 26,000-strong crowd and didn't finish until 8.42pm on the longest day of the English summer.

THE AFTERMATH

Tony Cozier wrote that the tournament was "perhaps the boldest and most ambitious innovation the game has known since the legalisation of overarm bowling". He wasn't wrong. The game has changed beyond recognition with the advent and growth of limited-overs cricket and is on the brink of another seismic shift following the birth and explosion of T20 franchise cricket. Where it will go from here, whether it will be for better or for worse is uncertain.

THE MEN IN GREEN

WORLD CUP GROUP MATCH

ENGLAND
VS
IRELAND
2011

PLAYED AT:
M CHINNASWAMY STADIUM,
BANGALORE,
INDIA

RUN UP TO THE GAME

Ireland's journey towards Test status had been gathering pace for a few years before they played England in the 2011 World Cup in Bangalore. They had gradually become one of the best Associate sides in the world over the first decade of the 2000s and had gained huge acclaim in the 2007 World Cup with a stunning win that knocked Pakistan out and also a win against Bangladesh. They had also knocked Bangladesh out of the 2009 World T20 and won their third successive Intercontinental Cup event in 2008. Adding spice to the matter was the ICC's decision to reduce the next World Cup to 10 teams from 14, making it difficult for Associate teams like Ireland to even qualify.

England, meanwhile, were nobody's idea of favourites going into the World Cup and were still in their decades-long struggle of figuring out how to play 50-over cricket. That said, they were comfortable favourites going into the match against Ireland.

THE GAME

England were in control of the match for most of it. They compiled 327-8 from their 50 overs and might have made more but for some good death bowling from Ireland. Kevin Pietersen bludgeoned 59 off 50 balls from the top of the order, while Jonathan Trott and Ian Bell put on 167 for the third-wicket. Trott made a run-a-ball 92 and Bell an 86-ball 81. The final 33 balls of their innings following Trott's departure yielded a disappointing 39 runs as John Mooney and Trent Johnston took late wickets.

Ireland's innings started in the worst possible way as William Porterfield dragged a James Anderson delivery onto his stumps first ball. Ireland did recover to some extent as Paul Stirling, benefitting from being dropped, made a brisk 32 off 28 balls and Ed Joyce and Niall O'Brien chipped in. Joyce was probably Ireland's best batsman and had played for England in the 2007 World Cup before being dropped and switching back to play for the land of his birth. His dismissal for 32 as the second man to fall in a Graeme Swann triple-strike, followed shortly afterwards by Gary Wilson's for 3 to make it 111-5. This looked to have sealed the game for England, but Kevin O'Brien would produce one of the best innings in World Cup history.

He didn't have much time as Ireland needed 217 off 154 balls following Wilson's departure and O'Brien had only the lower-order for company. He thumped Swann through the covers for four on the second ball and hit the off-spinner for two sixes in a single over to underline his intentions. The batting powerplay was then taken by Ireland. It had proved to be a relatively ineffective gimmick since the ICC had brought it into the 50-over game in an effort to spice it up in 2008. O'Brien soon rendered it very effective indeed and led the way as 62 runs came off the 5 overs, in the process bringing up his half-century off only 30 balls.

O'Brien's second 50 would be even quicker as he smashed Australian Matthew Hayden's previous record for a World Cup hundred of 66 balls to bring up his three figures off only 50 deliveries. He had survived a difficult swirling chance when in the 90s but Andrew Strauss had put it down and celebrated his hundred by removing his helmet to reveal some very purple hair – part Ireland's charity fundraising campaign.

The impressive Alex Cusack was run out for 47 off 58 balls in the next over, having more than played his part in an incredible sixth-wicket stand of 162 off 103 balls that had well and truly bought Ireland back into the match and well and truly rattled England.

If England hoped the new batsman Mooney would prove easier to deal with they were soon made to think otherwise. After taking a couple of overs to get going, he dominated the scoring during a breezy seventh-wicket stand that took the runs required down to just 12 from the final 2 overs. Surely Ireland couldn't lose it from here?

The first ball of the 49th over saw O'Brien run out as he desperately tried to get 2 runs where there was only 1. It was left to the vastly experienced Johnston to partner

Mooney. He immediately calmed nerves by hitting a full toss from Stuart Broad to the boundary and Ireland got it down to needing only 3 off the final over. It only took Mooney 1 delivery as he hit James Anderson through midwicket for 4 to cue wild celebrations.

THE AFTERMATH

Ireland failed to make it through to the next stage as they lost all of the rest of their group games bar the expected win over the Netherlands. England did qualify following close wins over South Africa, Bangladesh, and the West Indies before they were thrashed in the quarter-finals by eventual runners-up Sri Lanka.

Ireland's rise would continue and they beat the West Indies in the 2015 World Cup before being granted Test status in 2017 and playing their first Test against Pakistan in 2018. O'Brien would become one of Ireland's best ever players and not announce his retirement until 2022.

England would finally begin to take 50-over cricket seriously and won the 2019 World Cup under the leadership of their Irish-born captain Eoin Morgan.

The ICC, under much pressure, reversed their decision to restrict participation in the 2015 World Cup to 10 teams and it was again a 14-team affair.

AN UNEXPECTED TRIUMPH

WORLD CUP FINAL

AUSTRALIA
VS
SRI LANKA
1996

PLAYED AT:
GADDAFI STADIUM,
LAHORE,
PAKISTAN

RUN UP TO THE GAME

Sri Lanka were seen as underdogs leading into the 1996 World Cup but did not lose a match on their way to the final. They were still a relatively new international cricket team but were rapidly improving under their determined captain Arjuna Ranatunga. They had won their first overseas Test match only a year earlier and had impressed on a highly controversial tour of Australia a few months before the World Cup.

On that tour, Australian umpire Darrell Hair had called Sri Lankan spinner Muttiah Muralitharan for throwing, meaning that he was bowling illegally. Whatever the rights and wrongs of that decision it soured relations between the Sri Lankan and Australian teams ahead of their meeting in the 1996 World Cup final.

Sri Lanka was also in the midst of a civil war and had actually been awarded 2 of their group games by default after Australia and the West Indies had refused to travel to play there due to security concerns. The country's cricket team had never even made it out of the group stage in a World Cup before and they were up against a side who had won it in 1987.

THE GAME

It was with this background of civil war, controversy, and being underdogs that Ranatunga won the toss and asked the Australians to bat at Pakistan's Gaddafi Stadium. It soon looked like Australia would live up to their favourites tag as they breezed past 100 for the loss of only 1 wicket thanks to their captain Mark Taylor and fresh-faced future captain Ricky Ponting. However, Aravinda de Silva removed both and the innings faltered to 170-5. A useful 36 not out from Michael Bevan saw them reach a middling 241-7 from their 50 overs. De Silva ended with 3-42 with his off-spin as Sri Lanka's spin quartet that also included Muralitharan, Sanath Jayasuriya, and Kumar Dharmasena excelled.

Sri Lanka's success in the tournament to date had in part been driven by the aggression of Jayasuriya and Romesh Kaluwitharana at the top of the order in their role as "pinch-hitters". Unfortunately, they both fell cheaply in the final to severely dent their side's hopes. At 23-2, Australia were back in front.

Nonetheless, surely inspired by a partisan crowd that coach Dav Whatmore later estimated were 90% on their side (possibly due to them having defeated Pakistan's arch-rivals India in the semi-final in front of a furious Indian crowd), de Silva and Asanka Gurusinha rebuilt the innings. The pair put on 125 before the latter was out for 65. That was to be Australia's last success as Ranatunga and de Silva found the Australian bowlers increasingly to their liking and they eased to victory. De Silva became the first player not from the West Indies to hit a century in a World Cup final and ended on 107. He was an easy choice for man of the match following his 3 wickets earlier in the day. Sri Lanka, who had only won 4 matches in their previous 5 World Cups, were now champions having not lost a match.

THE AFTERMATH

The result announced Sri Lanka's arrival as a truly competitive international team in spectacular fashion. They would go on to reach the final again in both 2007 and 2011 but have suffered a worrying dip in form in the more recent past. The success of their pinch-hitting strategy marked another chapter in the evolution of one-day cricket.

Sri Lanka's captain Ranatunga later told BBC World Service at an event to mark 25 years since the triumph that the win was one of the best things to happen to him in his life and that "nobody expected us to win a World Cup" but that he had cricketers who "were more keen on doing justice for their country than themselves."

Australia recovered as Australia always do and had a period of absolute dominance that included winning the next 3 World Cups and 4 of the next 5.

CORNERED TIGERS

WORLD CUP SEMI-FINAL

PAKISTAN VS NEW ZEALAND 1992

PLAYED AT:
EDEN PARK, AUCKLAND,
NEW ZEALAND

RUN UP TO THE GAME

New Zealand had won 7 consecutive games during the group stage before losing – ironically – to Pakistan in their final match. They easily topped the table, setting up a home semi-final at Eden Park.

Pakistan's qualification had been much more difficult. They had been bowled out for just 74 by England before rain intervened and meant the match was abandoned and had won only 1 of their first 5 games. Ahead of their must-win 6th match against Australia, their captain Imran Khan, sporting a tiger shirt, is supposed to have delivered a speech that likened the Pakistan team to cornered tigers. According to Aaqib Javed, Khan said: "wounded tigers get angry, don't get disappointed." Speaking to the The National in 2015, Javed credited this speech with securing victory. Other players have dismissed the speech's importance and some can't even remember it taking it place. Whatever the truth, it has found a place in Pakistani cricket legend because of what followed.

THE GAME

New Zealand's captain Martin Crowe, whose decisions during the final were to play such a big part, won the toss and elected to bat. He later indicated to Cricinfo that the rain that was forecast for the afternoon and the tournament's eccentric rain rule that heavily disadvantaged the side batting second (and saw the other semi-final a day later end in farce) played a part in his decision.

The home side were favourites but started poorly, crawling to 87-3 after 24 overs. New batsman Ken Rutherford also struggled to get going. Crowe recalls: "He took a long time to get off the mark - I think he took 25 balls or so, which is an extraordinary amount of time to get off the mark." Rutherford did pick up the pace and reached his 3rd fifty of the tournament off just 65 balls. Crowe had also passed 50 and was on 81 when, attempting a run, he pulled his left hamstring. He was allowed a runner but lasted only another 10 runs when, as so often happens with a runner, a mix-up resulted in him being run-out.

Nonetheless, New Zealand had managed 262-7: a total that Crowe reckoned was 25 runs more than required and one that would allow him to rest his hamstring ahead of the anticipated final. John Wright would lead the side in the field.

Wright, though, did not know Crowe's meticulously worked out bowling plans and made several moves that Crowe did not agree with. It worked fairly well at first as Pakistan slowly subsided to 140-4 following the double loss of Imran Khan for a painstaking 44 and Saleem Malik for 1. They needed an imposing 123 from the final 15 overs and Javed Miandad had the fresh-faced and palpably nervous Inzamam-ul-Haq for company. Miandad later wrote in his autobiography that Inzamam "seemed nervous and overawed and looked like he had seen a ghost." It was later revealed that Inzamam had been forced by Khan to play despite a dodgy stomach. "Khan just told me to play my natural game," Inzamam told The Cricket Monthly. "It just so happened, whatever I tried that day was coming off." And come off it did as he played a match and career-shaping innings of 60 off 37 balls.

According to Crowe, Wright visited the New Zealand dressing room early on in Inzamam's innings for a toilet break and asked for advice. He was given some. Wright decided not to take it, meaning all-rounder Chris Harris had to bowl in the last 5 overs. "The writing was on the wall," according to Crowe.

New Zealand did have a good chance heading into the final 5 overs, however, as Inzamam was run out just before and 36 runs off 5 overs was still tricky. Pakistan, though, did not look back and Moin Khan hit the winning runs with an over to spare to finish on 20 off 11 balls.

Miandad played the anchor role superbly and finished unbeaten on 57 off 69 balls. Harris conceded 72 runs off his 10 overs. The rain that Crowe was told would arrive at 2.30pm did not arrive until 7pm.

THE AFTERMATH

Crowe took the blame for the defeat. "I had that dilemma of whether to go out on the field and captain the side and probably rule myself out of the final appearance if we made it," he said, "or to rest up and think that we had enough and I could kill two birds with one stone by not fielding."

Despite the defeat, Crowe would build on his reputation as an astute New Zealand captain and became a highly-regarded writer and commentator following his retirement. Wright, with a successful playing career already behind him, went on to have a successful coaching career, most notably as head coach of India.

New Zealand have still not won a World Cup.

Inzamam went on to become one of the Pakistan's greatest ever batsmen with more than 20,000 international runs. Khan's cricketing legacy was already secure and he retired after the World Cup with both it and his leadership reputation – partly due to that speech – enhanced. He went on to become Prime Minister of Pakistan.

A WIN FOR THE PEOPLE

WORLD TWENTY20 FINAL

ENGLAND VS WEST INDIES 2016

PLAYED AT:
EDEN GARDENS, KOLKATA, INDIA

RUN UP TO THE GAME

Both England and the West Indies had won the World T20 before: England in 2010 and the West Indies in 2012. Both sides had had relatively comfortable paths to the final, having lost only once all tournament: England to the West Indies in their first group game and the West Indies a surprise defeat to Afghanistan in a dead rubber final group game.

West Indies cricket was on a bit of a roll: their Under-19 side had won the World Cup earlier in the year, while their women had won the World T20 earlier that day. The one blot was that the players had almost boycotted the tournament altogether owing to a pay dispute with the West Indies Board.

England were competing strongly in limited-overs cricket consistently for the first time in what seemed like living memory.

The stage was set for a thrilling final.

THE GAME

West Indies were an excellent side batting second in T20 cricket and would have been pleased that their captain Darren Sammy won the toss to allow them to do so again in front of a huge Eden Gardens crowd. The match looked like being rather one-sided initially as England's top-order struggled, especially against the quick leg-spin of Samuel Badree who was the most economical bowler of the tournament. They quickly slipped to 23-3 following the loss of their captain Eoin Morgan.

Joe Root and Jos Buttler rescued things with an excellent partnership of 61 in less than 7 overs before Buttler succumbed to Carlos Brathwaite (more of whom later!). Root shepherded the other batsmen for a while before becoming 7th man out with the score on just 111 attempting to scoop Brathwaite over Sulieman Benn at short fine-leg. David Willey struck a couple of pleasing blows and managed to get England up to a respectable 155-9 off their 20 overs. West Indies' bowlers had been mostly good, with the weak link their 5th bowler: Benn and Sammy sending down 4 wicket-less overs at a cost of 54 runs between them.

Morgan decided to open the bowling with Root's off-spin and it soon bore fruit. Root had Johnson Charles out off his 1st ball and the dangerous Chris Gayle out just 2 balls later. When Lendl Simmons was sent packing by Willey in the next over the West Indies were 11-3 and had made an even worse start than England.

Dwayne Bravo and Marlon Samuels began the repair job that Buttler and Root had for England. They found the going a little heavier and their partnership of 75 took almost 12 overs as Willey, Liam Plunkett, and Adil Rashid bowled tightly.

The pressure built up finally yielded results as Bravo was dismissed for 25 off 27 balls and was followed soon afterwards by Andre Russell and Sammy to leave the West Indies on 107-6 and staring at probable defeat.

Enter Brathwaite to partner the superb Samuels, who had brought up his fifty off 46 balls. By the time Brathwaite took strike, the West Indies needed 40 off just 21 balls. That came down to 27 off 12 balls with Samuels on strike. 4 came off the first ball but only a further 4 from the next 5 to leave a stiff ask of 19 off the final over to be bowled by Stokes to Brathwaite.

Brathwaite recalls Samuels' advice ahead of the final over: "Swing for the hills!" Speaking to ESPNcricinfo, Brathwaite said, "I had an idea of Ben Stokes' plan simply because of the dimensions of the ground. Chris Jordan was trying to bowl wide yorkers, forcing us to hit to the longer end. So obviously Stokes was trying to bowl straight and get us to hit leg side."

The first ball from Stokes was angled down leg and was flicked by Brathwaite over fine-leg for six. The next was more on target but went whistling over mid-wicket for another six. The West Indies were now favourites but Brathwaite didn't let up. The third ball also went for six, over long-off.

Brathwaite recalled: "And that's when I realised: we needed one off three. I saw the West Indies women's team chanting. They had stayed back to watch us after winning their final. My girlfriend was in the stands. Marlon was going up and down. The phones were up, the camera lights were on. To be that person who had created that hysteria - you don't often get those days on such a big stage where you can be the main man. It was time to soak it in."

There was to be no change in method from Brathwaite as, despite only 1 run needed, he launched the 4th consecutive 6. The West Indies had won an incredible match with 2 balls to spare. Brathwaite finished with 34 off just 10 balls, with Samuels, who had already played the defining knock in the West Indies' 2012 triumph, named man of the match once again for his 85 off 66 balls.

THE AFTERMATH

The West Indies were unable to defend their title in the tournament held more than 5 years later, winning only 1 match. Brathwaite and Samuels didn't even make the West Indies squad, with Brathwaite's most recent appearance for them coming in 2019. He continues to play T20 cricket for various teams around the world. Samuels last played for the West Indies in 2018 and retired from professional cricket in 2020.

England reached the semi-final in the 2021 tournament, failing in their efforts to add the T20 title to the 50-over title they had won in 2019. Stokes would go on to become perhaps the greatest all-rounder in the modern game at present and was appointed England Test captain in 2022.

LAUNCH OF A REVOLUTION

WORLD TWENTY20 FINAL

PAKISTAN VS INDIA 2007

**PLAYED AT:
NEW WANDERERS STADIUM,
JOHANNESBURG,
SOUTH AFRICA**

RUN UP TO THE GAME

The remarkable growth of Twenty20 cricket, which was invented as a professional sport by the English Board in only 2003, was kick started by the highly successful inaugural edition of the T20 World Cup held in 2007. India's Board was initially sceptical of the format – some of their biggest name players did not play much T20 cricket – as they were doing very nicely out of 50-over cricket, while the first T20 international in 2005 was taken as a bit of a joke as Australia and New Zealand played in retro kit and some players sported 1980s hair and moustaches. T20's influence was beginning to be felt by 2007 as a group of entrepreneurs in India were trying to set up a Twenty20 league much to the Indian Board's disapproval.

India and Pakistan have a long rivalry in cricket and had played out a thrilling tie in the group game of the 2007 tournament, prior to India's win in the bowl-out tie-breaker. India did lose their opening super 8s match on their way to the final but qualified to play Pakistan, who won all 3 of their matches.

THE GAME

India won the toss and chose to bat first but were forced to make a change at the top of the order due to an injury to talismanic opener Virender Sehwag. His replacement Yusuf Pathan got his side off to a flying start in making 15 off 8 balls. However, the scoring slowed following his departure as India's middle-order struggled.

Yuvraj Singh, who had enjoyed such a wonderful match against England, hitting Stuart Broad for 6 sixes in an over en route to 50 off only 12 balls, was totally becalmed and could manage only 14 off 19 balls. Opener Gautam Gambhir did a wonderful job of keeping India's innings going in making a fluent 75 off 54 balls, while Rohit Sharma added an unbeaten 30 off 16 balls to help them to a total of 157-5 from their 20 overs. Umar Gul finished as the best bowler for Pakistan with 3-28, while Sohail Tanvir and Mohammad Asif took a wicket apiece.

Pakistan were probably favourites at half time but lost Mohammad Hafeez in RP Singh's opening over for just 1. Singh then got Kamran Akmal in his next over for a duck. In between these dismissals, however, Sreesanth's first over had been pummelled for 21 runs by Hafeez's opening partner Imran Nazir to mark a thrilling start to the run chase and highlight the all-action nature of Twenty20 cricket.

Sreesanth soon bounced back and delivered a maiden over before seeing Nazir run out to make it 53-3. Pakistani wickets continued to tumble and they were soon seemingly out of the contest at 77-6 following soon-to-be Man of the Tournament Shahid Afridi's dismissal for a first-ball duck. Misbah-ul-Haq remained the last hope for Pakistan and he kicked into life in spectacular fashion, hitting 3 sixes from the 17th over bowled by Harbhajan Singh. That made it 35 needed from 18 balls and 2 sixes in the next over by new batsman Sohail Tanvir made it 20 needed off the final 2 overs.

RP Singh bowled an excellent first 5 balls in the 19th over, conceding only 1 run off the bat and 3 runs in all before culminating in the removal of Umar Gul's leg-stump. Unfortunately for Singh, last man Asif carved the final ball of the over away for 4 to leave Misbah on strike for the final over and only 13 runs needed. It was anybody's game.

Events soon made Pakistan favourites as Misbah deposited Joginder Sharma back over his head for 6 to leave them needing only 6 from the final 4 balls. Next ball, however, Misbah tried to scoop the medium-pacer over Sreesanth at short fine-leg and only succeeded in giving him a simple catch. Pakistan were all out and India had won the first ever T20 World Cup by 5 runs. Irfan Pathan was named man of the match for his excellent spell of 3-16 from 4 overs.

THE AFTERMATH

The Indian Board, now fully aware of the impact of T20 cricket, announced a bonus of nearly US$200,000 for each player. They had committed to a new T20 league called the Indian Premier League just days earlier. This league, known as the IPL, would quickly grow into a multi-billion dollar endeavour and be copied by several other cricket Boards across the world. The effects of this on the wider cricketing landscape are only just beginning to be understood.

Pakistan's fans were understandably displeased by their team's loss but won the next edition of the tournament in 2009. India have not won again despite the monetary success of the IPL.

"WE MURDERED 'EM"

TEST MATCH 1996

ZIMBABWE VS ENGLAND
1ST TEST

PLAYED AT:
QUEEN'S SPORTS CLUB,
BULAWAYO,
ZIMBABWE

RUN UP TO THE GAME

England were only a mediocre Test side in 1996 and had won only 1 Test all year, losing 3 and drawing 3. Zimbabwe had fared even worse and had lost 3 and drawn 3 during 1996. They would have been ranked 9th and last in the Test rankings had they existed at the time and had only gained Test status in 1992. England had played their first Test in 1877.

With all that in mind, England were firm favourites as they embarked on their first full tour of a country which had only formally gained its independence from the UK in 1980. England's Board had also been the only 1 to vote against Zimbabwe gaining Test status; facts which perhaps contributed to the determination of the Zimbabwe players. England's players were also unhappy at the decision by their Board not to allow their wives and girlfriends to accompany them on the tour which took place over Christmas.

THE GAME

England did have the better of Zimbabwe for much of the game which made the end result and the later comments of coach David Lloyd more than understandable. With that said, Zimbabwe played well. They managed 376 after winning the toss and electing to bat as Andy Flower made a marathon 112 off 331 balls and captain Alastair Campbell making a brisker 84 off 136 balls. Robert Croft delivered 44 overs of off-spin for England for figures of 3-77 to lead their spin attack on a pitch that favoured it.

England responded strongly and had 2 century-makers of their own in Nasser Hussain and John Crawley. Both men took their time and Crawley was later criticised by some for his method of batting with the tail on the 4th day. Nonetheless England gained a small lead in making 406. By stumps on day 4, their bowlers had reduced Zimbabwe to 107-5 — a lead of only 77. Most assumed that England would win comfortably on day 5.

Zimbabwe, however, were not done fighting. Andy Waller and Guy Whittall made dogged half-centuries to lift Zimbabwe's total to 234, despite 4-61 from Croft's spin partner Phil Tufnell, and take valuable time out of the match. England were finally left needing 205 off 37 overs at a run rate of over 5.5 per over.

Captain Michael Atherton, not renowned for his fast scoring, delivered a mixed blessing by chopping on early in England's reply to leave the way clear for the faster-scoring pair of Nick Knight and Alec Stewart.

David Hopps in The Guardian wrote that: "Knight's willingness to risk the unorthodox provided initial impetus, while Stewart bossed and bristled like an army captain, never more so than with a straight six off Paul Strang."

England had got the equation down to 87 from the last 15 overs with 9 wickets still in hand and were firm favourites. Zimbabwe's bowling, though, began to get increasingly negative and the scoring rate slowed. Wickets also began to fall as Stewart's innings ended at 73 off his 76th delivery when he skied a catch to Campbell off Strang. Hussain survived only 1 ball before succumbing to Strang off his 2nd, while Crawley and Thorpe were also ineffective.

Knight was England's only hope left and managed to get it down to 13 needed off the final over. He hit the 3rd ball for 6 to reinvigorate English hopes. The 4th ball was so ridiculously wide that Knight "would not have reached it with an extension" but Zimbabwean umpire Ian Robinson, who Hopps wrote had "an embarrassing match" declined to signal a wide. Zimbabwe's Andy Flower later admitted to Cricinfo that "It (the wide bowling) was the right thing to do but it wouldn't be allowed to happen now. We were never going to bowl England out, so we had to make sure they couldn't get the runs."

England eventually ended up needing 3 from the final ball. Knight said, "I thought I had hit it for four and won the match. But it slowed up in the outfield, we scrambled through for 2 and I was run out going for a crazy 3rd."

The match was over and scores were level. It was the 1st time in the 1,345 Tests played to that date that such a result had occurred.

THE AFTERMATH

England's players were unhappy at the way that Zimbabwe had bowled in the final hours of the match and were also frustrated at the loss of play to rain on the 2nd day. This frustration was summed up by coach David Lloyd in comments that have entered into cricketing legend: "We murdered 'em...we flipping hammered 'em." He was given a ticking-off by Board chairman Lord MacLaurin, who flew in especially to deliver the reprimand. England were also reprimanded by the match referee Hanumant Singh for their aggressive appealing to add salt to the wounds.

As for Zimbabwe, with some fans angered by the comments from Lloyd, things only got better. They skittled England for 156 in a rain-ruined 2nd Test to draw the series. They then, remarkably, whitewashed England in the 3-match ODI series, with "chicken-farmer" Eddo Brandes becoming the 1st Zimbabwean to take a hat-trick in the 3rd match.

THE TIMELESS TEST

TEST MATCH 1939

ENGLAND
VS
SOUTH AFRICA
5TH TEST

PLAYED AT:
KINGSMEAD, DURBAN, SOUTH AFRICA

RUN UP TO THE GAME

England had embarked on their tour of southern Africa in 1938 surely unaware of what was about to bedevil the world. As was common in those days, they played a series of matches against local teams prior to the Test matches; the first of which began on Christmas Eve. The first 2 Tests were drawn, with England winning the 3rd by an innings and then drawing the 4th to set up a series finale in Durban. As the series was still live, the teams agreed that the 5th Test would be played without a time limit – the 99th and last time this would happen.

The 2 sides almost certainly expected the match to end in the usual 5 days as England had their final tour game scheduled for 11th March before they were due to sail home. Surely no one expected South African player Ken Viljoen to have 2 haircuts during the match or for the match to feature quite so prominently in the then-unfounded The Guinness Book of Records for decades afterwards.

THE GAME

The toss was historically very important in a timeless Test so the home crowd were delighted when South Africa's captain Alan Melville called correctly using teammate Norman Gordon's "lucky" coin.

With plenty of time, South African opener Pieter van der Bijl took 45 minutes to get off the mark and batted throughout day 1 for an unbeaten 105. Dudley Nourse took even longer over his 103 and was still at the crease on Monday 6th March en route to what was the slowest Test century at the time.

"It was a timeless Test, with no need to get on with the scoring," Nourse told Cricinfo shortly before his death in 1981. "My attitude was, the longer we batted the more runs we would score. That way we should probably win. So I felt they would just have to prise me out."

South Africa were finally dismissed on Monday (Sunday having been a rest day as was the case at the time) for 536. England then made only 316 as wicket-keeper Les Ames top-scored with 84 and leg-spinner Eric Dalton took 4-59.

South Africa's batsmen then carried on from where they had left off in the first innings; particularly van der Bijl who withstood some testing pace bowling from England's Ken Farnes. He had reached 97 and was a shot away from becoming the first South African to hit centuries in both innings of a Test match when he lobbed a simple catch to Eddie Paynter and had to trudge off.

Three South African wickets fell with the score on 191 after openers van der Bijl and Bruce Mitchell had put on that many for the 1st wicket. Legendary Yorkshire spinner Hedley Verity took 2 of them and would bowl 766 deliveries in the match. Any English hopes of a major collapse were soon dashed as Viljoen hit 74 and Melville 103 to haul South Africa up to 481 and leave England needing a surely-improbable 696 for victory.

Amos confided many years later that: "No one on the England side even considered we could get 696. But when [John] Edrich scored a double-century, and the scoreboard read over 400 for 2, the whole team was saying 'We can win this match.'"

Indeed, it was captain Wally Hammond's inspired decision to promote the 22 year-old Edrich that kick-started England's run chase. They overcame the loss of Len Hutton for 55 to close on Friday 10th at 253-1. There was then rain on Saturday and a rest day on Sunday, meaning that Edrich would resume day 9 on 107 not out.

Despite the length of the game and the growing threat of war back in Europe, the crowds remained engrossed by the game. Men formed groups and discussed the topics of the day, such as the gathering war clouds," wrote cricket writer Louis Duffus, "while little bands of women found themselves making remarkable progress with their knitting. 'See you tomorrow' was the popular farewell parting."

Edrich was finally dismissed for 219 shortly after a couple a glasses of champagne at the tea interval, but England pressed on to close on 496-3.

By this point, time in the timeless Test was beginning to run out as England had a train and boat, Athlone Castle, to catch back to Southampton so Tuesday would have to be the last day. Hammond and Paynter took the score past 600 as the storm clouds began to gather. Hammond was eventually stumped for 140 with the score on 650. The clouds emptied themselves minutes later and the decision was taken to abandon the game with the score on 654-5. The timeless Test had run out of time. Far more importantly, so had efforts at peace in Europe. On the 15th March, Nazi troops invaded Czechoslovakia.

THE AFTERMATH

Three of the players involved in the match – Ken Farnes and Hedley Verity from England, and Arthur "Chud" Langton of South Africa – would lose their lives in World War 2. John Lazenby wrote in his 2017 book on the match of the "the jarring juxtaposition of play ticking over at the pace of a grandfather clock winding slowly down, while Europe hurtled inexorably towards war." He added: "The Durban timeless Test of 1939 was the final gasp of a cricketing epoch, a sparkle of innocence and glamour that disappeared forever."

Many things changed as a result of the war. Timeless Tests were already being criticised and were probably on their way out but the war arguably ensured that they were another, albeit vanishingly insignificant, casualty.

The match remains the longest ever in Test history at 10 days (or 43 hours and 16 minutes of playing time) and the 1,981 runs scored remain the most ever in a Test match. The 766 balls sent down by Verity has only been exceeded once since, while Gordon's 738 deliveries remain the most bowled by a fast bowler in Test cricket. By way of an appropriate historical anomaly, The Times pointed out that legendary cricket statistician Bill Frindall was born on the 1st day of the match.

THE 438 GAME

ODI MATCH 2006

AUSTRALIA
VS
SOUTH AFRICA
5TH MATCH

PLAYED AT:
NEW WANDERERS STADIUM,
JOHANNESBURG,
SOUTH AFRICA

RUN UP TO THE GAME

South Africa and Australia have had an intense cricketing rivalry since at least the 1999 World Cup and the former's infamous last over implosion. It was fair to say that Australia had been having the upper hand in the months leading up to this match as they dominated the Proteas on their tour Down Under. The return match-up had been going better for the South Africans at home as they triumphed in the tour-opening T20 match and shared the 4 ODIs to set up a series decider at the Bullring in Johannesburg.

THE GAME

Australia won the toss and their captain Ricky Ponting elected to bat. The 2 openers, Adam Gilchrist and Simon Katich, immediately set the tone with a stand of 97 in little more than 15 overs. Gilchrist was eventually well caught by Andrew Hall off Roger Telemachus for 55 off just 44 balls, but this only bought Ponting to the crease.

Incredibly, Ponting would not depart until the total had passed 400 — something that had never been done before in ODI cricket. Along the way, he shared a partnership of 119 with Katich (79 off 90 balls) and the innings-defining one of 158 with Mike Hussey. The latter came off fewer than 16 overs and was ended only when Hussey lobbed a catch to long-off attempting his 4th six to bring his innings to a close at 81 off 51 balls.

Ponting reached his 150 off only 99 balls, a world record at the time, before falling for 164 off 105 balls, having smacked 13 fours and 9 sixes. Andrew Symonds hit an unbeaten 27 off 13 balls to take the total to a surely-insurmountable 434-4.

The South African bowling card was a mess. Telemachus had had respectable figures of 1-47 off 8 overs at 1 point, but a disastrous over at the death which contained 4 consecutive no-balls and yielded 28 runs for the Australians meant his final figures of 2-87 were very bad, although far from exceptional. Jacques Kallis delivered 6 wicket-less overs for 70 runs and is said to have quipped at the interval: "Come on, guys: it's a 450-wicket. They're 15 short!"

Many a true word is spoken in jest.

The hosts lost Boeta Dippenaar early in the run chase, but skipper Graeme Smith and Herschelle Gibbs added 187 inside 21 overs as their side began their quest for the distant summit.

Smith was out for 90 off 55 balls, while Gibbs only narrowly missed out on breaking Ponting's record from just hours earlier by bringing up his 150 off 100 balls. He was finally out for 175 off 111 balls, while the losses of Kallis for 20 and Justin Kemp for 13 left South Africa with plenty to do at 355-6 in the 43rd over. Australia were probably favourites but in this incredible match it was anyone's guess.

Johan van der Wath whacked 3 sixes in 5 balls to keep South Africa on track and pushed the score up to 399 before falling for 35 off 18 balls. It all came down to the final over and 7 needed with 2 wickets left. Mark Boucher was still there for South Africa and batting well and he had all-rounder Andrew Hall for company.

Boucher took a run from the 1st ball. Hall smashed the 2nd for 4. Surely that was it? No, Hall was out of the 3rd, attempting the winning hit. Suddenly, Makhaya Ntini – a great bowler, but a very poor batsman – was on strike. Calm as anything, he hit a single to bring the scores level and to leave Boucher 2 deliveries to hit the winning run. He only needed 1 and drove the ball over mid-on for 4. South Africa had won a remarkable match and broken a world record set only hours earlier with their humungous total of 438-9.

In an unusual move, Ponting and Gibbs were both awarded the man of the match award. The game itself is still remembered fondly by cricket fans, particularly South African ones, and is sometimes known as "The 438 game". Newspapers at the time called it the greatest ODI ever.

One-Day cricket continues to produce higher and higher scores, but South Africa's winning total remains the highest ever run chase. The total of runs scored by the 2 sides of 872 also remains the highest, whereas the match aggregate of 26 sixes has since been beaten. Australian fast bowler Mick Lewis retains the unwanted record of most runs conceded in an ODI with 113. He was dropped from the Australian squad following the match and sadly never played for them again.

Remarkably, the Australians proved very resilient. Just 4 days later they bowled the South Africans out for 205 in the 1st Test and went on to whitewash them 3-0.

Printed in Great Britain
by Amazon

19409194R00068